A Few Poetic
Conversations

and

Some Other Works

Volume 2

ISBN: 979-8-9850173-0-4

How to read this *recueil* of poems?

As with the first book, I want to foster and further the love of poetry. Poetry is not static. It changes with the passage of time and with people. However, the wide range of emotional experiences never changes. In this optic, a poetic conversation can be elicited, continued, and arrived at a consented end through the works of the authors.

When able, in respect to copyright and other laws, I have included the original works - the start of the conversations - followed by the response.

Garry F. Doxy

Table of Content

Some Other Works

Garry F. Doxy
Engine Number 4*

In the rain
and darkness
Engine number 4
sped up
steaming
firing
slippery
…
tragedy
for it trued up not
to the flashing red light inside the brume.

*Please refer to William Carlos William's *The Great Figure*

Paul Laurence Dunbar
A Changing Time

The cloud looked in at the window,
And said to the day, "Be dark!"
And the roguish rain tapped hard on the pane,
To stifle the song of the lark.

The wind sprang up in the tree tops
And shrieked with a voice of death,

But the rough-voiced breeze, that shook the trees,
Was touched with a violet's breath.

Garry F. Doxy
A Song for The Times

How triumphant is a calming love.
It clears the onlooking clouds far up above
And from the tree tops dries the birdlime.
It stops the "roguish rain" from drowning
The brown passerine which has been voicing
The free song of the hour - a changing time

Garry F. Doxy
Yes! The Days Are Full Enough*

Yes! The days are full enough of malfeasance.
Yes! The nights are full enough of egotists.
And, yes! Life carries on despite everyone;
  Not even making a dent in the cruelty of
some.

*Please refer to Ezra Pound's *And The Days Are Not Full
Enough*

Alfred Edward Housman
**Poems From "A Shropshire Lad" - XIX - To
An Athlete Dying Young**

The time you won your town the race
We chaired you through the market-place;
Man and boy stood cheering by,
And home we brought you shoulder-high.

To-day, the road all runners come,
Shoulder-high we bring you home,
And set you at your threshold down,
Townsman of a stiller town.

Smart lad, to slip betimes away
From fields where glory does not stay
And early though the laurel grows
It withers quicker than the rose.

Eyes the shady night has shut
Cannot see the record cut,
And silence sounds no worse than cheers
After earth has stopped the ears:

Now you will not swell the rout
Of lads that wore their honours out,
Runners whom renown outran
And the name died before the man.

So set, before its echoes fade,
The fleet foot on the sill of shade,
And hold to the low lintel up
The still-defended challenge-cup.

And round that early-laurelled head
Will flock to gaze the strengthless dead,
And find unwithered on its curls
The garland briefer than a girl's.

Garry F. Doxy
They Are Dying Young !

No true words ring so sadly:
They are dying young ! As many
We chaired under the arena's lights,
As many trembled after through the nights.

Their tributes are so smartly deserved.
Their sublime feats we eagerly preserved
In sound bites, highlights, and the rest.
More! More! More! We sternly jest.

Gladiators wearing the scented bays
Of sacrifice, your mindful days
Are dancing like a mirage beyond
The mark. Should you break the bond?

The unbridled enemy comes like a thief.
Upon the butte, wold, jebel, the feudal chief
Cuts the runner down with its heather crown
And drags his grandeur into to the ground.

Now, no more cheering, elated lads!

Now, no more dazzling, supercut ads!
Only, on the long list of those we have lost,
They have vanished quickly in the minds'
frost.

So, passingly futile it is to be: the glory,
Think of the future, of God's paternity,
Think of harmony between man and beast,
Work at and for peace, at the very least.

Look at the twisted faded garland vines;
Listen to the eulogium, the dirge's lines:
They are fading young! Blooms of Spring
Unfurling, iridescent, muting, and dying,

Samuel Butler
Hypocrisy

Hypocrisy will serve as well
To propagate a church, as zeal;
As persecution and promotion
Do equally advance devotion:
So round white stones will serve, they say,
As well as eggs to make hens lay.

Garry F. Doxy
By All means

Because of the white stone
To hypocrisy some are prone.
Lime-washed tombs they are;
Illegitimated, unrighteous by far.
By all means, eyeing the One seat,
They will sink like Stone Fleet.

Robert William Service
Fi-Fi in Bed

Up into the sky I stare;
All the little stars I see;
And I know that God is there
O, how lonely He must be!

Me, I laugh and leap all day,
Till my head begins to nod;
He's so great, He cannot play:
I am glad I am not God.

Poor kind God upon His throne,
Up there in the sky so blue,
Always, always all alone . . .
"Please, dear God, I pity You."

Garry F. Doxy
He is Not Alone

On a throne He does sit,
As fittingly as He should be.
After all, He is the Almighty.
You were given that wit.

Because of the very first boy,
All his stars began shouting
Together: What a joy! Yes, joy!
He also as a father was reveling.

You, laughing, leaping all day,
And when nodding, to sleep
You go. "He cannot play", you say.
Watch a parrot, a cat, a sheep...

Garry F. Doxy
He Fits in Perfectly*

How does he fit in?
With the life, the grin
He has, the rum he drinks,
The many words he thinks,
The mandated how-do-you-do,
The passions and deceptions too.
He fits in so perfectly when so many
Are destroying, ruining, acting insanely.

*Please refer to Malcolm Lowry's *Eye-Opener*

Some Other Works

Sonnet pour Hélène
by Pierre de Ronsard
– Sonnets for Hélène
Translated and Interpreted
by Garry F. Doxy

When you will be old, at night, by candlelight,
Sitting near the fire, unwinding and spinning
You will say, in wonder, my verses singing :
Ronsard celebrated me when I was so bright.

You'll not have servants, awaiting intimations,
Already half asleep and tired just the same,
Awakened upon hearing news of my name,
Venerating you with immortal acclamations.

Being interred and a boneless phantom surely,
Under the dull shadows, I will rest miserly ;
And you will be a bent old lass by the fire,

Lamenting my love and your proud disdain.
Enjoy life, believe me, do not abstain.
Pluck now the roses of life, do not tire.

À qui la faute?
by Victor Hugo
Who's to Blame?
Translated and interpreted
by Garry F. Doxy

"You just burn down the Library?"
"Yes."
"I lit a match to it."

-But that's a crime, a senseless…!
An infamous crime committed against
humanity
And yourself! You just took out the only
Beacon for your soul! You put out your
lantern!
What your insane and wicked rage dared to
burn
Is your dower, treasure, property, your
heritage.
The book, authors' ogres, is to your
advantage.
The book has always fought for you, gone to
bat

For you. A library is a supremely religious act
From generation of men who were without
light,
Who still offered homage to the coming
twilight.
What! In this fusion of truthful sincerity,
In these masterpieces full of gusto and clarity,
In this mausoleum of time, a repository,
In the centuries, in primitive men, in history
In the past, of lessons learned hereafter,
In things that began and will last forever,
In the poets! What, in this chasm of *Biblos,*
In the terribly divine writings of *Aiskhylos,*
In the Homers, the Jobs, lining the horizon,
In Molière, Voltaire, Kant, sowing reason,
You started, wretched man, a bonfire!
Of all the spirit of man you made a smoking
fire!
Have you forgotten who liberated you?
Books! The book is through and through
There on the hill glistening, shining, revealing;
And the scaffold, wars, famines: eliminating.
It speaks, no more slavery, no more pariah.
Search a book. Plato, Milton, Beccaria.

Dante, Shakespeare, or Corneille, read these
prophets
The breath of their soul will offer to you
possets;
Although dazzled you feel the same as they
do;
In reading you become pensive, benign, anew;
You feel these great men in your intellect
grow;
That the dawn enlightening a recluse, they
show
As long as they drive deeper into your heart
The warm rays that sooth and a light to
impart;
Your questioned self is ready to respond to
them then;
You agree see and see yourself as good, better
even,
You feel the snow, your arrogance, your ire,
Your prejudices, wrongs, kings, emperors melt
in the fire!
Because science in men came first
Then liberty. All this enlightened thirst
Belongs to you, understand, and you
extinguishes it!

Your dreaming goal the book realizes it.
The book enters your mind, separates truth
from rot,
Because all consciences are in a Gordian knot.
It is your doctor, your guide, your guardian.
To you now hatred and madness are alien.
That is what you have lost, alas, by your
doing!
The book is your very treasure! It is leaning,
Rights, truth, virtue, progress, reason chasing
Away all hysteria, incoherence, all raving.
And you destroyed all of it!

"I never learned how to read."

Garry F. Doxy
A White Speck

The smell of a brimful coffee
Woke up all lives, even an infant tree.
It came from a white speck that grew
From the green, mossy valley. A few
Chatty rabbits argued it a stork;
The flies buzzed: the Cathedral of York;
A wolf snarled and wished it a tasty thigh;
The birds sang: maybe a giant firefly
For it smokes and glows at night;
It's beaming eyes scare you outright.
Then, the air descended to zero or below;
The speck disappeared in the falling snow.

La Colombe et la Fourmi
by Jean de la Fontaine
The Dove and the Ant
Translated and Interpreted
by Garry F. Doxy

Along a clear streamlet a Dove was supping,
When an ant fell in the water, upon reaching;
And in that ocean, one could see
The ant trying, but in vain, to reach the shore.
The Dove quickly wielded charity:
In the water, a blade of grass she dropped
instantly,
It was an escape, a headland, and more.
The ant is safe; but then
Here was coming a certain barefoot
highwayman.
This good-for-nothing brigand had a
crossbow.
As soon as he sees the Bird of Venus, the
cateran

Saw it in his pot and already feasting for the
morrow.
When our brut of a man took aim for the
sorrow,
The ant bit him at his heel, right away.
He turned his head; the dove had a friend in
tow;
And hearing him, she decided to fly away.
The villain's super disappear without
summation;
No Dove for a donation.

Le Mur

by Guy de Maupassant

The Wall

Translated and Interpreted

by Garry F. Doxy

Through the opened windows, the "salon's"
light
Burned, on the grass, life's brightness casually
Mingling inside in a rhythmic cadence aright.
The park, there, seemed answering strangely
The orchestra's melodies. The lukewarm
nocturnal
Air carried earthy and woodsy scents, vernal
Breath, the odors of perfumed bodies, and hay
Stroked the exposed shoulders. The uplifting
air
Hushed the candles' flame. The mistic play

A Few Poetic Conversations v. 2|Garry F Doxy

Of odorous flowery fields, cleverly stacked
hair,
A crisp cold wind from the sky- punctured by
Mars
And crossing the shadowy lawn- brought the
dust of stars.

The women, sitting lazily, eyes widen, silent
Watched, and time to time, like wind beaten
sails,
Dreamed of a journey across the golden
firmament.
A longing, a need to suppress all soulful ails,
To love, to say with tenderness all the
romantic
Elans that a heart can imprisoned. The music
Lulled and seemed perfumed; the night
drummed

And permeated the air and you heard the
wails
Of stags. But, through the whitened skirts
hummed
A shiver. All departed and the musical aside
Stopped. Behind the woods' darkness, on a
hillside,
The moon, enormous and red, rose as a
sweeping
Fire through the evergreens. Rounding and
rising
In the faraway ether, she went up lonesome
Like a ghostly face wandering away from
home.

All scattered on shadowy trails, where the
moon,
On white sand, on a dormant pond, was
scattering

A Few Poetic Conversations v. 2|Garry F Doxy

Her charming light. The tender night was
making
Lovers out of men with incendiary stares and
soon
The women, serious, head bent, were feeling,
a little of that moonlight deep under their
skin.
The gentle, incensed, winds were prodding
the listless bodies into the slow dance of sin.

Ambling, and without knowing why, happy,
a little giggle swinged me around, then
suddenly
Appeared the lady I love, Alas! discreetly for
never
Has she returned my adoring, devoted fervor,
And loving wishes. She said in the dark:
"Your arms, and let's take a turn about the
park."

She was a free, vivacious, and opiniated
friend.
She professed that the moon was husbandless:
"That the trail is too long to see it to the end
Because I have delicate shoes and that my
dress
Is new. Let's turn around." I took her away
swiftly
By the arm. So, she ran freely and insouciant,
And the wind from her dress, randomly and
violently
Scattered the dormant air. Then, winded and
spent,
she stopped; and silently we went down an
alley.
We heard tender voices speaking in the night
And amongst the movements, of which the
dark

Was populated, one could distinguish the
light
Sound of a kiss. She would make a remark
At the sky! Quickly silence fell. A lite flitting
Was heard. And a few jaded lovers
imprecated
The disruptors. A nightingale, nearby, was
singing
and a quail, in the distance, in the plain
riposted.
Suddenly, a white wall, whose cutting
reflection,
chased the darkness; and as in a fairy tale,
stood
a metal palace. From a distance, a peculiar
attention
it seemed to have paid to us. It said: "Light is
good
For those wanting to stay blameless. At night

Too dark are the woods. Let's sit on that sight,
In front of that wall so bright." She sat
laughing
Seeing me cursing her. In the deep sky,
grinning
The moon seemed to be. And both, in concord,
We're settling to spread between friends a
discord.

In front of the pale wall we were sitting,
hence;
And I dared not to say: "I love you!" But since
I was suffocating, I took both of her hands.
Her lips twisted slightly and to make amends
Allowed me to come close like a patient
hunter.
At times, the dresses passing on the shadowy
paths made each for a doubtful white figure.
The moon hid and engulfed us with its silvery

Rays, and melted our hearts at its tender face.
She was gliding way high, very slowly,
placidly
And invaded our flesh with a languorous
embrace.

Observing my companion, I felt in my senses,
in my soul, in my shaken being this fever
of desire which from women cause us to
quiver!
It is like, each night, in idolizing trances
We dream of the consenting kiss with closing
eyes,
The yes requited; like the adorable ingenue
whose garb we touch; the abandoned flesh
that lies
In our arms immobile and spent. To be true,
The lady only gives us a feeble moment
To seize and to hope for a blissful torment.

A Few Poetic Conversations v. 2|Garry F Doxy

My throat was dry and my teeth were
grinding
From the ardent tremors that came running,
Like the fury of a slave in revolt; and with the
joy
That my strength could be used as a ploy
To lay hold of this haughty and serene woman
And make her jolt and jump like a showman.

Laughing haughtily, mocking beautifully,
Her breath created a fine vapor
Of which I was thirsty. My heart jumped; folly
Took over me. I took her in my arms. She was
in horror
And got up. I grabbed her waist in vexation;
Her arched nervous body underneath me, I
kissed, with flair,
Her eye, her forehead, her moist lips, and her
hair.

A Few Poetic Conversations v. 2|Garry F Doxy

The moon, triumphant, giddy, shined with
admiration.
Though I was loving her, impetuously and
strongly,
I was repelled, through a supreme effort,
forcefully.
Then, was restarted our frantic fracas,
Near the wall that seemed like a large canvas.
Having stopped and turned around abruptly
We witnessed a strange and comic spectacle.
Tracing two unfettered bodies and unsoundly
In the open, our shadows projected a comical
Play alternating: pulling, pushing, and
embracing.
They seemed to be playing some buffoonery
With crazy pantomimic gestures full of fury.
The surges of Love these scenes were
portraying,

twisting, convulsing, interlocking horns,
suddenly
Standing, revealing their true heights or
deploying
Four gigantic arms instead. A tug of war,
incidents
That were seen black on the wall, on its
whiteness
And displaying a sudden a grotesque
tenderness
and being swooned in burning amorous
moments.
This situation being fun and very unexpected
She began to laugh – And how can you be
angry,
Tussling and stopping lips to get closer, get
acquainted
When you laugh? A moment of desperate
hilarity

Can better save a lover than a heart burning
with desire.

The nightingale was singing in his tree. The
moon, vainly,
In the serene sky, searched for two shadows
full of fire
On the wall, but witnessed only one in total
harmony.

Garry F. Doxy
A Castle on the Sand

From 1859 or 1861, beyond 1865, in May,
The Dixie daughters dressed in blueish gray
Have yet loved even a man for they kept
Eating, burning the fat and the blood and
wept
Their lost golden age. Guns willed, even
buried-
More precious than lost lives; hands were
hurried
Because of the menacing and devasting steel.
All of those sacrifices were…are under the feel
Of the pyramid's watchful eye. A certain
Green
Colored everything it saw and sadly it has
been
A grinding machine for men and nature.
Led by a *deus* instead of the Divine, the future,
Under the power of a crescent iron hand,
Became a glistening castle built on the sand.

Mon Rêve Familier
from Poèmes saturniens

by Paul Verlaine
My Familiar Dream
Translated and Interpreted
by Garry F. Doxy

Of an unknown woman whom I love and
who loves me,
I often have this penetrating and strange
dream
and at one moment or another who
doesn't seem
To be one thing but still loves and
understands me as it should be.

For she knows me and my heart, clear
without fears
For her only, alas! cease to be a mess
For her only; and from my pallid forehead,
the moistness

Only her knows how to replenish with her
tears,

Is she a brunette, blond or redhead? I'm
unknowing.
Her name? I remember it to be sweet and
sounding
Like that of the beloved ones that life
dispossessed.

Her stare is like that of the marble carvings
And her voice is distant, calm, and grave;
she possessed
The inflexion of the voices that are now, to
the dear departed, siblings.

Le ciel est par-dessus le toit
from Sagesse (Book III, VI)
by Paul Verlaine
Above the Roof
Translated and Interpreted
by Garry F. Doxy

The ether is, above the roof,
Cerulean, so calm!
A tree is, above the roof,
Fanning his palm.
A bell, in the sky we see, aloof,
Softly dings.
A bird on the tree we see, aloof,
Plaintively sings.
My God, my God, life isn't a spoof,
To tranquility and simplicity.
That conceivable rumor, a spoof,
Comes from the city.
What have you done, O you, a goof,
Crying ceaselessly.
Say, what have you done, you, a goof,
Of your youth's vitality?

Orphée I
from Le Bestiaire: ou Cortète d'Orphée
by Guillaume Apollinaire
Orpheus I
Extract translated and Interpreted
by Garry F. Doxy

Admire the remarkable ability
And the pedigree of the nobility:
It is the voice that the light aired
And of which, in his Pimander, Hermes
Trismegistus declared.

The Turtle.

Of magical Thrace, O what satire!
My steady fingers play the lyre.
To the sounds of my turtle, of my songs
Marched the animal throngs.

The Horse.

My formal dreams will know how to
mount you,
My destiny on a golden chariot would be
your coachman too
Whom for reins will hold with ecstasy
My rhymes, the paragons of all poetry.

The Goat of Thibet.

The skin hairs of that goat, and even
The golden one that labored Jason
For, do not possess the worth
Of the hairs that I am enamored with.

The Serpent.

You target beauty relentlessly.
How many women were mercilessly
Victims of your cruelty!
Eve, Eurydice, Cleopatra and more;
I know of three or four.

The Cat.

I wish to have in my homestead
A woman with a solid head;
Among the books, a cat walking;
Friends, not by seasons led,
Without whom life is not worth living.

The Lion.

O lion, an unfortunate image:
Kings have failed miserably;
Now, you start life in a cage
In Hamburg, in Germany.

The Hare.

Do not be afraid and lascivious
Like the hare and the amorous.
But let your brain be of some worth
Like the pregnant hare that is giving birth.

The Rabbit.

I know of another bunny
Which alive I would like to catch.
Among the dells of Tenderness country,
Among the thyme it does hatch.

The Dromedary.

With only four dromedaries
Don Pedro d'alfaroubeira, who
Traveled and admired their armies,
Lived as I would have like to do
If I also possessed four dromedaries.

The Mouse.

Beautiful days: time is smiling.
Mouse, you nibble at my life slowly.
God! I will be eight and twenty, aging
And lived I believe so horribly.

The Elephant.

Like an elephant's ivory,
I have a mouth full of things - precious.
Purple death!...I price my glory
With the value of words – melodious.

Aubade parisienne
from Cahier Rouge
by François Coppée
Parisian Aubade
Translated and interpreted
by Garry F. Doxy

For the love of you, my dear,
I crossed white runlets;
And so, my heart in fear
I even pitied pullets.

What is the time then ? It is frosting.
I could believe it is Spring.
Do you hear, Mademoiselle?
You returned to me my twenties so well.

My eyes shine again.
This heart I felt once past,
For you, it has life to gain;
Listen, how it beats even at rest.

A Few Poetic Conversations v. 2|Garry F Doxy

What is the time? Lunch time:
Take this fruit and have a bite.
It's fine. We are at our prime,
And I will feast on your teeth so white.

Tell me, say something.
I'm only seeing and deaf by choice.
Move your rosy lips so thin
And I will inhale your voice.

I love and love you more;
At your feet I do submit.
Let me have a go at it; I adore
The soft boudoir's rug I admit!

Also, by this author:

A Few Poetic Conversations & Some Other Works (First book)

Emile & Irisa (a short novel)

www.ingramcontent.com/pod-product-compliance
Lightning Source LLC
Chambersburg PA
CBHW070452130626
46553CB00006B/2374